INNER THOUGHTS OF A STABLE GENIUS

POEMS BY JERERMY GULLEY

Kansas City Missouri

Spartan Press
Kansas City, MO
spartanpresskc.com

Copyright © Jeremy Gulley, 2020
First Edition1 3 5 7 9 10 8 6 4 2
ISBN: 978-1-952411-16-8
LCCN: 2020937850

Author photos: Fredrick Kegoda, Jackson Kapkayai
All rights reserved. No part of this publication may be reproduced or transmitted in any form or by any means, electronic or mechanical, including photocopying, recording or by info retrieval system, without prior written permission from the author.

Acknowledgments:

Acknowledgments: I would like to thank Beth Gulley, Dan Krause, James Benger, and Jason Baldinger for being sounding boards for these poems. I would like to thank Asher Gulley for the idea — *A madman never worries if they are one...no stable genius would call themselves a stable genius.* Many thanks to Israel Gulley for keeping me supplied with new music. Thanks, also, to *365 Poems in 365 Days* and Alien Buddha Press for daily inspiration. And finally to Spartan Press for finding these poems worthy of print.

TABLE OF CONTENTS

#1 / 1
#2 / 2
#3 / 3
#4 / 4
#5 / 5
#6 / 6
#7 / 7
#8 / 8
#9 / 9
#10 / 10
#11 / 11
#12 / 12
#13 / 13
#14 / 14
#15 / 15
#16 / 16
#17 / 17
#18 / 18
#19 / 19
#20 / 20
#21 / 21
#22 / 22
#23 / 24
#24 / 25
#25 / 26

#26 / 27
#27 / 28
#28 / 29
#29 / 30
#30 / 31
#31 / 32
#32 / 33
#33 / 34
#34 / 35
#35 / 36
#36 / 37
#37 / 38
#38 / 39
#39 / 40
#40 / 41
#41 / 42
#42 / 43
#43 / 44
#44 / 45
#45 / 46

To all the stable geniuses
masquerading as madmen.

*I was born not knowing
and have had only a little time
to change that here and there.*

— Richard Feynman

Inner Thoughts of a Stable Genius #1

on this cold in mid-winter day
we'll hunt ghosts on our walk
go to the local coffee shop
and find a coffin full of bones
be served with morning tea
by tight, white, rigid men
and maids in dark dresses,
tall and graceful men and women
with names and surnames
that will surely outlast them

Inner Thoughts of a Stable Genius #2

I need to laugh but I'm makin' soup

I'm hungry but I've been sniffin' glue

I am a free man but I can't tell a joke

so tell me a joke, I need to laugh

but not the one about, you know,
how I try to look up to people like me

Inner Thoughts of a Stable Genius #3

when I came around again

the kettle went on

the clean towel we took to the sink

was dry before we finished our cups

Inner Thoughts of a Stable Genius #4

— Good Morning Mr. Rabbit —
ah, how soft you would lie when you're asleep,
and how easy it is to wake up like the day before!
there are of course things to be learned from every event
and the *Morning Bell* proves that.
I'll ask our beautiful parrot:
what did your sister ask for this morning?

Inner Thoughts of a Stable Genius #5

the children

carried air

to the summit

to find

the enemy,

and when the

first shot came,

it was their

childhood

that was shot

in the head

Inner Thoughts of a Stable Genius #6

the cold, the storm and the rain,

in vain, the warning cries

of the priests, the *sting-nose* drums,

out of all this pain and loss

in vain the prayer of the wounded

Inner Thoughts of a Stable Genius #7

another world is coming down around us

and I'm not willing to get in its way

I'm not willing to let it all go

if the medium is the message

then I might as well get the message out there,

so I'll dance my way through the world,

a movement far more potent than I thought

Inner Thoughts of a Stable Genius #8

the daydreams of a foreigner

a dog in an office on a wire

you're being asked what you've done

but you're already done

and plan to do it agaiin

Inner Thoughts of a Stable Genius #9

a time of crisis,

or discontent,

should awaken someone

to revive the country's soul,

Inner Thoughts of a Stable Genius #10

know there's people out there like me

they say the only way out is in

that walk through hell to get there . . .

I know there's something wrong with me

I'm a selfish wreck in a prison of my own making

I'm a demon but they don't see me

I'm a mirage but they don't see me

yeah I'm the broken sign that keeps turning

and my tale is written by a crazy Christian boy

but we're here to all meet on the cross

and tell our lies on the cross and still
no one can deny the truth

yeah I'm the broken sign that keeps turning

and my tale is written by a madman

Inner Thoughts of a Stable Genius #11

to make this displeasure known

someone on this Earth must be your friend
especially in the face of this risk

it seems that here in God's Country
it's safer to go alone

Inner Thoughts of a Stable Genius #12

somewhere
to someone in the night

will still be heard
a question

– What are you doing?

– And what are you feeling?

– Is he alive?

– Can we go?

– What are we doing?

– What's happened to him?

and they will float to the sky
where the pilots will catch them
and the pilots can tell you a million things
– then you'll be able to tell them a million things
– then they'll tell you a million more things
– they'll be three million things then.
you can never go beyond three million things.
that's the way it's gonna go with these guys.

Inner Thoughts of a Stable Genius #13

and his tattered writings
and their mother's empty lies
and fine ladies
and the dear people of the village
don't all know that "Before You Give It All Away" is
a fool's song
they just can't bear to hear
they won't trust a word you say
they won't put up with it
but at least they say that
but what they don't say
is: they can't even trust the word *All*
when it says *We're all, together, together, in the world.*
the damn fool has his holy day
but who's the fool now?

Inner Thoughts of a Stable Genius #14

for a place near a full moon, for a pool of quiet water, there are few alluring attractions.

even without a redhead who loved nothing more than frolicking in the mud, the village came back.

ah, I see you don't want to talk about the princess, you want to ask something about our village.

did I mention that there's a full moon tonight? And a fountain of milk the size of a single thumb?

yeah, that's a big deal.

speaking of a *big deal,* it's something that's going to be the root of our eternal enmity.

we won't talk about it again.

Inner Thoughts of a Stable Genius #15

as I said, there is no wrong side to the coin,
no need to delve into the muck for answers,
just pick up the two sides of the coin, mark
one side *right*, and mark the other *wrong*
and at that point, you are ready to do the
math on the exact value you will end up with

Inner Thoughts of a Stable Genius #16

was his first class condition,
whose mind he was himself unhealthily altered
with worldly opinions and wanton aims;
mere circumstance, Pater, did assign,
whose prediction he trusted not;
which though dire, yet he trusted rather
to be a visionary to himself.

such joy and wondrous surprise
made virtue smile, when he met
the ideas of great perfection
(whose contrary he dreaded) then
of supreme imperfection.

it is thus from the first he did strive
to advance towards vice:
while he wished he could sink in it.
conceited nature not

Inner Thoughts of a Stable Genius #17

by the light of a dying sun!
naughty, naughty, we
found you hidden in the woods.
now from under the dock you look
into our wood and tell us what
you know.

saying it's no sin to take
from the books of conscience
the naked dogma of hell:
and to *press* (make this word start
to sound in an English idiom),
from the abandoned urchins
the lazy beheaders of Christ,
unworthy of humanity.

Inner Thoughts of a Stable Genius #18

once they killed the flowers,

chankokich, chankokich,

the forest cried for vengeance

Inner Thoughts of a Stable Genius #19

so my writing must die
and I must put on writing clothes.
but what joy is there in facing the unknown
when I know better than to face
it, itself, when I look inside
the flesh and bone of its angel's soul?
her life was the door

Inner Thoughts of a Stable Genius #20

no more than the moonflowers in the moon

through the daybreak's quickening gale withers
or in the evening firelight, another rung up the ladder,
will the last bell ring, will the wretched angels sing
I know you now, and, for truth, know you to certainty

Inner Thoughts of a Stable Genius #21

emotions too human to be handled,

man's fiery desires fixed only for love.

and, as a loyal lover is faithful,

he'd go to his death for his beloved,

and when he was dead, her abandoned and lost,

like the time when he first woke up beside her

in her old bed, she'd call to him,

still senseless of her own life,

for love was still alive in him to love.

but who could be more dead than a mind,

and lives only for fear of being dead?

and, through that mind's fiery passion

the sun is blind and fallen in the ocean

Inner Thoughts of a Stable Genius #22

Words that should be used as curse words with meanings derived by the perpetrator and/or victim, from only one section of the alphabet:

Dirtyenalagh

Dohaih

Dride

Dupa

Dutriseth

Dutriseth (n)

E

Eonagh

Ettingham

Enland

Ettingham (n)

G

Gaciremac (n)

Gagrocem

Gaciremac (n) (ess)

Gachan (gakhan, gachan)

Garfirth

Gebrion

Gedagh

Gedhar, n.

Gedharr (n)

Gedharr (n)

Inner Thoughts of a Stable Genius #23

holy man! Wherefore, if they hear of it and do not believe

they say: I have heard that a man hath killed the Divine Prophet

as for myself, I have no wife or children; and these

of the peoples of the world are in the filthy habit of

practicing adultery and taking wives in violation of the

sex ordinance. They are worldly and vainglorious;

forgive my outburst if not. I will stand at a private place

and call upon God to witness what I have said. Wilt thou go

back to thy own family?

the Heavens belong to God. He is glorified and He is

praised.

Inner Thoughts of a Stable Genius #24

dancing into the bay at dawn

the sun is glowing on the wall

and every door is shut

since we sold our last cow

I feel that the fish are gone

censors surround us now

the lamp posts up on the wall

can't go near the water

it's just too threatening

serves us right for seeding an atomic bomb

that can explode and swallow all we know

though you will see them all and make sure

every time they've been on screen

to keep the face away

all we know is

they're here

and we've got to survive

Inner Thoughts of a Stable Genius #25

Roses are red
Violets are blue
Clovers are blue
Ginseng is white
Weeds are yellow
Chrysanthemums are yellow
Clematis is white
Lilacs are yellow
Marigolds are white
Lilacs look like the
miniature snowflakes
that are found in photos
of Southern Oregon
and raindrops?
Keep falling on my head.

Currently red.

Inner Thoughts of a Stable Genius #26

Yesterday, while the sky spit snow,
I submerged myself in the still waters
of a nearby lake, and as I was floating
on the ice's edge, I saw all the fish
swimming over the silver sky,
where one carried another,
one on the lake, the other the water,
the moon must have sold her sheets
to the sun during the night,
the ones that shine so
brightly on the ice, they seem to glow,
and I as I thawed my bones, I thought, now
here's a sport they'll never show on TV

Inner Thoughts of a Stable Genius #27

I will forgive as many
times as I feel like,
and if you think three
strikes you're out
also applies to relationships,
then I ask what other
aspects of your morality
are you taking from
a sporting activity .. ?

Inner Thoughts of a Stable Genius #28

Someone asked if the cat
had my tongue and I said
no, the cat and I are not
related at all, my older son
has a lot of my characteristics,
such as my eyes and jawline,
and my younger son resembles
me in numerous ways, making
us unmistakably father and son,
or at least people who saw
us would know we were closely
related, but I have not passed
any of my characteristics to the
cat, the least of which is my tongue

Inner Thoughts of a Stable Genius #29

In my quest for advice
on how to make the perfect
at home potato chip, I
read an article that says
*cut the potatoes uniformly
so they cook evenly* . . .
I say, outloud, to myself
and the cat, *fucking nazi,*
because it dawns on me, in
that moment, that what the
world really needs is a batch
of unevenly cooked potato
chips that aren't judged by
an arbitrary standard, but
appreciated for their uniquness

Inner Thoughts of a Stable Genius #30

Most days
Everyday
Today
I sit
For at
Least
Five
!minutes
With a
Gun hanging
From
My teeth
And to
Not pull
The.
Trigger I
Think
Tomorrow
Will
Be better
And up
Until
Now
I've
Been
Right

Inner Thoughts of a Stable Genius #31

I'm my time in China
I was told that the common
greeting which translates
to *have you eaten* in English
was a hold over from the
Revolution, when people
didn't have enough to eat
and were concerned about
their fellow citizen,
lately I've been greeting
people by asking,
Are you working? and
I can't help but wonder
if in 50 years people will
wonder where this
greeting came from

Inner Thoughts of a Stable Genius #32

The 2016 baseball Word Series,
which, come on, is actually
the United States Series, featured
the Cubs and the Indians, an all
American combo if there ever was
one — little bears and Native People . . .
but it also featured John Hirschbeck
in his last game ever, which should
not be an afterthought— he's a
legend and should not be forgotten —
but it also features me 1/2 way
around the world in Xi'an, China . . .
I missed it all, Ross, Heyward, Coghlan,
and all the missed chances before
the rain delay and the final out and
from where I was the phone call from
my son who said *dad, they did it . . ."*
and they did, but I couldn't celebrate,
until the Chinese man raised his glass
of rice wine to celebrate life instead
of baseball, but now, in the middle of
the pandemic, it plays as a rerun,
and I am able to relive the impossible
life I chose to leave behind

Inner Thoughts of a Stable Genius #33

In my dream I
followed a skeleton
rooster past a rock
quarry and, once past
the designated *do not
pass*, line, my companion
blew up like a bubblicious
bubble and left his guts
on the rocky walls,
I woke thinking how my
brother never paid back
or apologized
when I had to pay the
lawsuit he brought on against
our shared business after
spending thousands of
dollars on nefarious acts
and I wondered if it was
my forgiveness on the wall
or some other substance,
but either way it was a
quite satisfying dream

Inner Thoughts of a Stable Genius #34

Last night I dreamed
I was forced, kicking and
screaming as much
as is allowed in dreams,
to run for President of the US,
and I woke in a sweat,
knowing that any love I
still hold for myself would
vanish if I were, in fact,
someone who would want
that job, but in the sunlight
of the waking world, I'm
energized by the fact that
my psyche gave me such
an encouraging nightmare

Inner Thoughts of a Stable Genius #35

I've traveled my fair share,
around the US, China, Europe,
South America, and spent time
in Pakistan where everywhere
I went I was either encouraged to
stay behind a high fence or
accompanied by armed guards,
but the scariest place I've ever
been is the two mile stretch of
road between the glass plant
near my house, and the highway
people use to get to and from
the place they don't want to go,
are angrier when they leave,
and take it out on us poor folk
just trying to have a peaceful drive
with no desire to fight the mistreated,
unappreciated American working class

Inner Thoughts of a Stable Genius #36

When one door closes,
open it again, that's what
doors are meant to do,
can you imagine if we met
every closed door with
resolved defeat and skittered
off to find another door —
oh, I was going to have dinner
at home tonight, but Teresa has
closed the door, I guess I'll
try somewhere else instead,
too bad, of course it might just
be stuck, from sticky hands
pulling the handle too many times,
so you may need to pull harder,
or it might be locked, in which case
you should use a key to open it,
if you are on the outside, from the
inside you can just turn that little
mechanism and it should open
just fine, that how doors work

Inner Thoughts of a Stable Genius #37

A friend of mine
works at a daycare
and I said to him
*oh, cool, you get
to meet new people
all the time,* and
he says the classes
don't change much
but I say, *no, I mean
there are some new
people there, not as
new as at the newborn
floor at the hospital,
but still pretty new, how
great for you to get to
meet so many new
people,* and he reminds
me that his classes don't
change much, and that
the way I see the world
isn't necessarily the same
way that he sees it

Inner Thoughts of a Stable Genius #38

Listening to totomami by
Pony Bravo when the news
breaks that the government
isn't prepared for a pandemic
and I'm pleased that the most
confusing part of my day is
the colloquial use of totomami
and not the incompetence of
the government of the USA

Inner Thoughts of a Stable Genius #39

I could tell he was trying to sing.
His mom told me he used to . . . a lot,
until he got annoying, she said,
and I imagined her . . . remembering,
wishing he was annoyingly singing again
instead of the grunts that made up his
full vocal repertoire since his step-dad
locked him in the upstairs closet and
set the house on fire, and his mom,
having no other options, threw him
out of the window, and he landed face
down on the sidewalk . . . age 8.
But still, 10 years later,
I could tell he was trying to sing.

Inner Thoughts of a Stable Genius #40

when I came around again

the kettle went on

the clean towel we took to the sink

was dry before we finished our cups

Inner Thoughts of a Stable Genius #41

the cold, the storm and the rain,

in vain, the warning cries

of the priests, the *sting-nose* drums,

out of all this pain and loss

in vain the prayer of the wounded

Inner Thoughts of a Stable Genius #42

(Ondaatje's Elimination Dance cont.)
Any woman who uses the term *Hubs* in a non-ironic way
Any person who has spent 30 minutes or more in a cell
  phone store opening accessory packages with a hunting
  knife for phones they don't own and then leaves without
  buying anything
A person who has said they're paying with a g-spot when
  they meant c-note
English actors who take roles in American films and use
American accents
American actors who take roles in English films and use
  English accents
A university professor who puts a wax statue of herself in
  front of the classroom during final exams
Someone who cuts in line at the DMV
Guitarists who use the term *ax*
Anyone who judges others' grammar silently
People who don't enjoy puns
People who use too many puns
Small town men who work regular jobs and steal the
  girlfriend of big city lawyers when the girl returns home
  for the holidays
People who have punched a seal
Anyone who has had to be physically removed from the
  St. Louis zoo for touching penguins

Inner Thoughts of a Stable Genius #43

Someone told me today
that I should live my best
life . . . I smiled politely
and walked away, knowing
I would never speak to that
person again, both because
of that comment and because
I like my life the way it is,
jagged and mostly ill-advised

Inner Thoughts of a Stable Genius #44

I admit that I've
almost got in love
with that thing that you do
that's keeping me
wild —
on the face of the day
the pleasure is still all
that I need
if you just gave
me half that —
I swear it will be enough
and my tongue will just
slip out of my mouth
and that's all I want

Inner Thoughts of a Stable Genius #45

When faced with
the choice between
eating Cheetos for
breakfast and writing
a meaningful poem,
I will, if there is time,
be content with cleaning
cheese dust from my
keyboard and hope
that some wisdom
seeped in there somehow

Jeremy Gulley is a Kansas City based writer, teacher, musician, motorcycle enthusiast, adventurer, traveler, father, and husband. These poems were written during his time living and traveling within China, Kenya, and Pakistan.

www.ingramcontent.com/pod-product-compliance
Lightning Source LLC
Chambersburg PA
CBHW030139100526
44592CB00011B/959